Growing in

Grace

"but grow in the grace and knowledge of our Lord Jesus Christ" (2 Peter 3:18)

A Ministry of:
Striving for Eternity Ministries
www.StrivingForEternity.org

Growing in Grace

Lessons

1) Salvation: *Reconciliation with Our Lord*
2) Prayer: *Access to Our Lord*
3) The Bible: *Revelation about Our Lord*

> **Receiving His Grace**

4) Baptism: *Identifying with Our Lord*
5) The Church: *Serving Our Lord*
6) The Lord's Table: *Remembering our Lord*
7) Testing: *Persevering for our Lord*
8) Obedience: *Commitment to Our Lord*
9) Holiness: *Living like Our Lord*

> **Living His Grace**

10) Stewardship: *Offerings for Our Lord*
11) Evangelism: *Speaking for Our Lord*
12) Christian Home: *Legacy for Our Lord*

> **Sharing His Grace**

The Lord is not slack concerning His promise, as some count slackness, but is longsuffering toward us, not willing that any should perish but that all should come to repentance."
2 Peter 3:9

"but grow in the grace and knowledge of our Lord and Savior Jesus Christ."
2 Peter 3:18

1 Salvation

Reconciliation with Our Lord

What is your relationship to God? Your answer to this question is a matter of spiritual life or death. Some think they cannot know until they meet God. However, God, through His Word, has told all humanity the way to Him; and through His Son provided that path. This lesson will discuss the need, way, blessings, and assurance of salvation.

I.   THE NEED FOR A RELATIONSHIP WITH GOD

     A.   What is the spiritual nature of all men?

          Romans 3:10, 23; Isaiah 53:6 _____ (Also see Ecclesiastes 7:20; Isaiah 64:6)

          Ephesians 2:5 _____

     B.   How does God respond to sinners? (Psalm 7:11)

          "God is_____ with the wicked _____ _____"

     C.   What is the penalty God has placed upon sin?

          Romans 6:23 _____
          Revelation 21:8 _____

          Even though God is a loving God, He is also a holy God who _____ sin. Either a person's sins are covered by the sacrifice of Christ or they are exposed before God and He will judge them, because God will have no sin in His presence. (Psalm 5:4-5)

     D.   Is it possible to save ourselves? (Titus 3:5; Ephesians 2:8-9)

          _____

     E.   Who has provided a way for salvation? (John 3:16; Romans 5:8)

          _____

     F.   Who can be saved? (Romans 10:13; John 1:12)

          _____

II.   THE WAY TO A RELATIONSHIP WITH GOD

A.   Repent

"The Lord...is longsuffering toward us, not willing that any should perish, but that all should come to _____ " (2 Peter 3:9)

Repentance is simply turning away from whatever else you **trusted for salvation as well as your sin and turning to God**. It is a changing of your mind and a surrendering of your will. You cannot have a relationship with God if you do not see **your sin as severe in God's eyes**. It is a turning from sin and self and turning to God. One cannot turn away from sin and self without replacing it with something to turn to.

B.   Receive

What must one do in order to be considered a *"child of God"*? (John 1:12)

_____ _____

How does one receive Christ? (Romans 10:9-13) _____ and

_____.

If we see our need as a sinner and call upon God in prayer, believing that Christ died and rose again for us, receiving Christ as the Lord and Savior of our life, He said that we shall be saved!

When is the best time to receive Christ? (2 Corinthians 6:2; Isaiah 55:6)

_____

Have you ever received Jesus Christ as your Lord and Savior? _____
If so, when did this happen? _____

III.   THE BLESSINGS OF A RELATIONSHIP WITH GOD

A.   We are a _____ _____ (2 Corinthians 5:17)

B.   We _____ we have eternal life. (1 John 5:12-13)

C.   We can never be separated from the _____ _____ _____ once we become a Christian (Romans 8:34-39; John 10:27-30)

D.   Our sins are now _____ (Ephesians 1:7)

E.   If we have received Christ, we are now considered a _____
_____ _____ (John 1:12)

F.   We are now _____ of God and _____ _____
with Christ. (Romans 8:17)

G.   We now have the _____ _____ _____ dwelling within us
       (1 Corinthians 3:16; also see Romans 8:9 and Ephesians 1:13)

IV.   THE ASSURANCE OF A RELATIONSHIP WITH GOD

Can we be assured that we have salvation? When we become a child of God there are
certain evidences that assure us that we are children of God.

A.   We are **Honest** about Our Sin

       The truth is not in us if we say we have no _____ (1 John 1:8)

B.   We are **Obedient** to God's Word

       We know Him if we _____ His _____. (1 John 2:4).

C.   We are **Loving** Other Believers

       We are not in the light if we _____ our brother or sister in Christ. (1 John
       2:9)

D.   We do **NOT Love** the World

       If we love the world, what is not in us? (1 John 2:15-16)

       _____

E.   We are **Practicing** Moral Uprightness

       How are the children of God and the children of the devil manifested
       [revealed]? (1 John 3:10)

       _____

F.   We are Bearing **Spiritual Fruit**

       Read the fruit of the Spirit in Galatians 5:22-23. Do you see these qualities
       developing in your life? _____

Assignment: *Memorize 1 John 5:12-13*
                  Write your salvation testimony on the following page.

Write in the space below your salvation explaining your life prior to salvation, how you were saved, and how your life has changed after salvation.

2 Prayer

Access to Our Lord

Prayer is a very important part of the Christian's life. Its importance is seen in how much time Christ spent in prayer. Even though God knows our very thoughts, He desires for us to express our praise, gratitude and requests before Him (1 Thessalonians 5:16-18).

I.   WHEN SHOULD I PRAY?

Every born-again believer has the privilege of entering into the presence of God at any time. However, it is a good idea to set aside a special time and place for prayer each day (Psalm 55:17). Make this a private time as Christ did (Luke 5:16).

II.   HOW SHOULD I PRAY?

Christ's disciples had this same question in mind when they came to Him and said, *"Lord, teach us to pray"* (Luke 11:1). Christ responded by giving them a model prayer (Luke 11:2-4).

   A.   Pray **Reverently**

   When we pray we are to remember that God's name is _____ (Luke 11:2). The word *"hallowed"* means "to treat as holy."

   We should not approach God in a flippant or disrespectful manner, even though we can come to Him in the most intimate and personal way.

   B.   Pray **Submissively**

   We are to pray for _____ will to be done on earth (Luke 11:2)

   Jesus is suggesting that true prayer includes willing obedience to Him. If we are praying for God's will on earth, then we are to be doing God's will on earth.

   C.   Pray **Dependently**

   We should seek God for our daily _____ (Luke 11:3).

   This attitude includes both reliance upon the provision of God and contentment with what He has provided.

D.   Pray **Honestly**

To what extent can we expect Jesus to forgive us of our daily acts of sin? As we _____ others (Luke 11:4).

Christ taught that we should ask God to forgive us as we forgive others! When a Christian sins, he should confess and forsake that sin before God (1 John 1:9). If a Christian has sinned against another person, they are to seek their forgiveness before they seek God's forgiveness (Matthew 5:23-24; Matthew 18:15-18).

E.   Pray **Preventively**

We are to ask God to lead us away from any type of _____ (Luke 11:4)

Christ taught His disciples to ask God to direct them away from anything that would entice them to sin. When we pray, we should ask God to keep us from impure thoughts and actions.

Make a list of things you are tempted with that you know God wants you to change. Pray every day that God would lead you from these temptations (1 Corinthians 10:13)

III.   DOES GOD ANSWER PRAYER?

Yes, God will always answer the believer's prayer. This does not mean that He always gives the answer that we want. God answers with a "yes", "no" or sometimes "wait". God will hear and answer the believer's prayer, providing he prays in the following manner:

A.   If it is prayed in _____ name (John 14:6; 15:16; 16:23-24).

B.   If it is prayed in agreement with _____ will (James 4:3).

C.   If there is no _____ that may hinder the believer's fellowship with God (Psalm 66:18).

D.   If there is no unconfessed sins between you and your _____ that could hinder your prayer (1 Peter 3:7)

E.   If it is prayed in _____, believing God is able and desires to answer your prayer (James 1:5-7)

IV. WHAT ARE SOME THINGS WE ARE TO PRAY FOR?

Below are some Scriptures that either tell us some things to pray for, or show us what the writers of the Scriptures prayed for.

A. 1 Timothy 2:1-2 _____

B. 2 Thessalonians 3:1 _____

C. Philippians 4:6 _____

D. Matthew 5:44 _____

E. Psalm 51:1-4 _____

F. James 1:5 _____

G. Revelation 22:20 _____

H. Matthew 9:37-38 _____

I. 1 John 1:9 _____

J. Romans 5:1-3 _____

V. SOME PRACTICAL SUGGESTIONS

A. Write a list of the things above plus others in which you want to pray.

B. Use the list as a reminder when you pray.

C. Mark those things in some way that God has answered.

Assignment: *Memorize Philippians 4:6-7*
Write out a prayer list.

3 The Bible
Revelation about Our Lord

God has taken the initiative in arranging for fellowship with men by revealing Himself in three ways:

    1) Through Creation (Psalm 19:1-4)
    2) Through His Son (John 14:9)
    3) Through His written Word, the Bible (2 Peter 1:21)

Creation can only teach us about God's _____ and His _____ (Romans 1:20)

His Son is the fullest revelation of Himself that is possible (Colossians 1:19). During this age, however, Christ is not physically present to teach us objective truth. He thus has given us the Word of God (2 Timothy 3:16) and His Spirit to guide us in all truth (1 John 2:27).

We receive communication from God today through His written Word, the Bible. The Bible is God's authority to the world for faith and practice.

I.   INSPIRATION OF SCRIPTURE

    A.   It was inspired by _____ (2 Timothy 3:16).

         The word *"inspired"* means "to exhale, to breathe out". It is an act that takes place when one is speaking. All Scripture (from Genesis to Revelation) is from the breath of God. The Bible is the product of God spoken words.

    B.   Men were directed by the _____ _____ to write the Bible (2 Peter 1:21).

         The Bible was written by about 40 men over a period of about 1,500 years. These men included fishermen (Peter, James and John); scholars (Paul); poets (David and Solomon); prophets (Jeremiah, Isaiah, Ezekiel and Daniel); shepherd (Amos); kings (David, Solomon).

         While the Bible was written by men, it was the Spirit of God who used each of these men's personalities and surroundings to record all that is written, so that we may be assured that the Scriptures are God's word, without error.

II.   IMPORTANCE OF SCRIPTURE

By answering the questions below, a student of Scriptures may see exactly how important is God's Word.

A.   What does the Apostle Paul say is the power of God unto salvation? (Romans 1:16) _____

B.   What does the Bible say we can know for certain? (1 John 5:13)
_____

C.   What did the rich man's brothers need to believe in order to escape hell? (Luke 16:29-31)? _____
("Moses and the prophets" was one of the Jewish names for the Scriptures.)

D.   Job considered the Word of God more necessary than _____ (Job 23:12).

E.   We should desire the Word of God so that we may _____ (1 Peter 2:2).

F.   What, along with prayer, is our defense against spiritual warfare? (Ephesians 6:17) _____

G.   What did Christ use to defeat Satan? (Matthew 4:4, 7, 10) _____

H.   What effect will the Word of God have upon one's life? (Psalm 119:9, 11)
_____

I.   God's Word is more powerful than any _____ (Hebrews 4:12)

III.   INVESTIGATION INTO SCRIPTURE
A.   Why should we study it?

1.   We should desire the sincere milk of the _____ so that we may _____ (1 Peter 2:2-3).

2.   What do we need to hide in our heart to keep us from sin? (Psalm 119:9, 11) _____

3.   God's Word is profitable for (2 Timothy 3:16)

_____ – right thinking

_____ – wrong thinking

_____ – wrong actions

_____ – right actions

4.   Studying and obeying God's Word will result in the man of God being (2 Timothy 3:17):

_____

_____

B.   How Should I Read the Bible?

1.   Read it **daily**. (Acts 17:11; 2 Corinthians 4:16)

2.   Read it **obediently**. (James 1:22)

3.   Read it **carefully**. (2 Timothy 2:15)

4.   Read it **systematically**

It is important that we carefully and correctly interpret God's Word. When you approach the Scriptures, ask these questions:

a)   **Who** are the writers and recipients?

b)   **Why** did they write what they wrote?

c)   **When** was it written?

d)   **What** timeless principles may be learned?

e)   **How** do these principles best apply to your life?

C.   Some practical considerations for your private study:

a)   Plan a certain time each day to read.

b)   Begin with prayer.

c)   Underline, memorize or write down verses that have special meaning to you.

d)   Apply the Scripture you studied to life.

e)   Close in prayer.

IV.   INFORMATION ABOUT SCRIPTURE

A.   It is **trustworthy** (Ezekiel 12:25; Matthew 5:18)

B.   It is **eternal** (Psalm 119:89; Isaiah 40:8; Matthew 24:35)

C.   It is **not** to be **altered** (Deuteronomy 4:2; Proverbs 30:6; Revelation 22:18-19)

Assignment: *Memorize 2 Timothy 3:16-17*
Set up a daily time and schedule for Bible study

4 Baptism

Identifying with Our Lord

Baptism is a topic of the Bible that has been confused by many people. Our authority on the subject however is the Word of God. Therefore, we will ask the Word of God to explain what baptism is, why it is important, who should be baptized, when they should be baptized and how they should be baptized. The Bible will clearly answer all these questions.

I. **WHAT** IS BAPTISM?

Read Romans 6:3-4 and indicate below what these verses say baptism pictures.

A. Water baptism pictures our spiritual baptism into the _____ of Christ (Romans 6:3).

B. Water baptism pictures our _____ in death with Christ (Romans 6:4).

C. Water baptism pictures the _____ of Christ, which illustrates the truth that we are going to walk in newness of life (Romans 6:4).

Baptism is an **outward demonstration** of what took place inwardly at salvation. It signifies the spiritual death of the believer's old man of sin, the spiritual burial of the old man of sin and spiritual resurrection of the new man in Christ.

II. **WHY** IS BAPTISM IMPORTANT?

A. Because God **Commanded** it

"Go therefore, and make disciples of all the nations, _____ them in the name of the Father and of the Son and of the Holy Spirit." (Matthew 28:19).

B. Because the Apostles **Preached** and **Practiced** it

1. What did those who receive the Word do immediately after their conversion? (Acts 2:41) _____

2. What did the Corinthians do once they heard and believed on the Lord Jesus Christ? (Acts 18:8) _____

For a further demonstration of the importance of baptism in the early church, please read Acts 2:38; 8:38; 9:17-18; 10:48; 16:15, 33 and 19:4-5.

C.   Because it is a Public **Testimony**

The _____ and _____ came to observe the baptism of John (Matthew 3:7). Those who were being baptized demonstrated to these religious leaders their commitment to the message of John.

In the first century, the church baptized outside before the entire communities to testify publicly that they were now identifying with Christ (see Matthew 10:32-33).

III.   **WHO** SHOULD BE BAPTIZED?

A.   **Only** Believers

"...and the eunuch said, See, here is water; what hinders me from being baptized? ... And Philip said, if you _____ with all your _____, you may" (Acts 8:36-37).

The Bible never teaches that a man should be baptized in order to remove sin. Neither does it teach that a believer should be baptized to keep himself saved.

Baptism is **not** a sacrament that gives any type of grace to a sinner. It is an **ordinance** which is a demonstration to symbolize what has already taken place in the life of a person who has trusted Jesus Christ to be his Lord and Savior and identification as a follower of Jesus Christ.

B.   **Every** Believer (Matthew 28:19; Acts 2:41)

How many were saved on the day of Pentecost (Acts 2:41)? _____

How many were baptized on that same day? _____

Notice that **NOWHERE** in the New Testament is there a record of any an **INFANT** being baptized. It was only and always **BELIEVERS**!

IV.   **WHEN** SHOULD A BELIVER BE BAPTIZED?

A believer should be baptized as soon as possible. Read the following verses and write down how soon after salvation was a person baptized:

A.   Acts 2:41 _____

B.   Acts 8:36-38 _____

C.   Acts 16:14-15 _____

D.   Acts 16:30-33 _____

V.   **HOW** SHOULD A BELIEVER BE BAPTIZED?

A.   The word *"baptize"* comes from the Greek word *"baptizo"* which means to "dip, plunge, or immerse". In the sense of believer's baptism, it never means to pour or sprinkle, for these methods would never picture the memorials mentioned above.

B.   Why did John baptize near Aenon? (John 3:23)

_____

C.   Philip and the Eunuch went down both _____ the _____ and he _____ him (Acts 8:38).

We can see that these verses indicate that much water was necessary for baptizing. This would not be true if one was to pour or sprinkle.

Assignment: *Memorize Matthew 28:19-20*
Complete the following review on the next page:

Complete the following review on baptism.

1. What does baptism have to do with salvation? (Ephesians 2:8,9)

2. Do the waters of baptism wash away sin? If not, what does? (Hebrews 9:22; Ephesians 1:7)

3. Write down, in your own words, why a believer should be baptized?

4. How soon should one be baptized after receiving Christ as Lord and Savior? (Acts 2:41; Acts 8:26-40)

5. Have you ever been baptized the biblical way? _____

6. If no, are you willing to be baptized the Bible way? _____

5 The Church
Serving Our Lord

Many people often have a variety of questions concerning church membership. Some of the most frequently asked questions are: What is a church? Which church should I join? What criteria should I use as a basis for choosing a church? What are believers to do in the church? This study is designed to answer these questions from the Bible.

I.   DEFINITION OF A CHURCH

The word *"church"* in our Bible is used to translate the Greek word *"ekklesia"*, which names an assembly of people who have been "called out" of the community for a specific purpose. Nearly every time this word is used in the New Testament it is a reference to a specific group of people in a community who:

A.   Have all been born-again through faith in Jesus Christ.

B.   Have all been baptized by immersion as a testimony of their faith (Acts 2:41).

C.   Have separated themselves from the life of the world.

D.   Are committed to the building up of the saints and to the worship of the Savior (Ephesians 4:11-15; 1 Timothy 4:13-16).

E.   Establishes qualified pastors for the teaching and administration of the church and deacons for the service of the church (1 Timothy 3:1-13; 5:17; 1 Peter 5:1-4). Notice that the titles "bishop (overseer)", "elder", and "pastor" all refer to one office. See Acts 20:17-28; Titus 1:5-7; and 1 Peter 5:1-2.

F.   Reach the lost for Christ in local church evangelism and personal evangelism (Acts 1:8).

G.   Exercise godly love and biblical discipline over believers (Matthew 18:15-17; 1 Corinthians 5).

H.   Keeps itself pure from worldliness, false doctrine, and false teachers (2 Corinthians 6:14-18; Jude 3-4).

I.   Have a mutual love and concern for one another (Galatians 6:1-3).

II.   THE IMPORTANCE OF A LOCAL CHURCH

About 100 of the 106 times the word *ekklesia* is used it is referring to a LOCAL group of believers. The importance of local churches is seen in the following biblical facts:'

A. The Bible teaches that believers should not _____ the _____ of themselves. (Hebrews 10:25)

B. Believers in the New Testament were automatically added to the _____ (Acts 2:47).

Notice that there is no biblical record of a New Testament Christian who was not part of a local church.

C. The Church is to be the _____ and _____ of the _____ (1 Timothy 3:15).

D. The Church was given men gifted for teaching and pastoring so they could _____ the saints and they in turn could do the work of the _____ for the _____ of the body (Ephesians 4:11, 12).

E. All of the epistles (Romans – Revelation) were written with churches in mind, with the possible exception of Philemon.

F. Christ loved the _____ and gave Himself for it (Ephesians 5:25).

G. The Church is the God-ordained governing body over the activities of believers.

   1. They kept a roll of members (1 Timothy 5:3-16; Acts 2:41)

   2. They had officers (Acts 14:23; Philippians 1:1; 1 Timothy 3:1-13; Titus 1:5).

   3. They send out missionaries (Acts 13:1-3).

   4. They received funds for the support of the ministries and the needs (Acts 2:45; 1 Timothy 5:17, 18).

   5. They disciplined their members (Matthew 18:15-17; 2 Thessalonians 3:6, 14-15).

   6. They baptized and administered the Lord's Table (Acts 2:41-42; 1 Corinthians 11:17-34).

Notice that, while all believers are in the greater body of Christ, the local church was instituted by God to be the visible expression of that greater body which will be together at the end of the age. **No** invisible body can perform the duties above.

III.   THE PURPOSES OF THE LOCAL CHURCH

Each member of the body needs to be active in fulfilling the purposes of the church. What are the purposes of a local church?

A.   Worshipping God

1.   Acts 2:47 indicates that the entire church was *"_____ God, and having favor with all the people…"*

2.   Paul says that a priority in the church is to give on behalf of all men and leaders *"_____, _____, _____, and giving of thanks…"* (1 Timothy 2:1-2). These are all part of public prayer.

3.   A responsibility of the church is to *"give attendance to _____, to _____, to _____"* (1 Timothy 4:13). These three ideas all relate to the public reading and teaching of the Word of God.

4.   The church is to be teaching and admonishing one another through *"_____, and _____, and _____ songs"* (Colossians 3:16).

5.   In 1 Corinthians 16:1-2, the *"_____ for the saints"* was taken as a part of their worship time.

B.   Serving Fellow Believers

1.   Through **Participating** with Fellow Believers

In Acts 2:41-42, once they *"received the Word"* there were six activities that each of the Christians participated in. What were they?

(1)   _____

(2)   _____

(3)   _____

(4)   _____

(5)   _____

(6)   _____

2.   Through **Ministering** to Fellow Believers

The *"one another's"* of the New Testament provide for each believer instruction on the importance of ministering to other believers. Read the following verses and list how we can minister to one another.

a)   Romans 15:14 _____

b)   Galatians 5:13 _____

c)   Galatians 6:1 _____

d)   Galatians 6:2 _____

e)   Ephesians 4:32 _____

f)   Ephesians 4:32 _____

g)   Ephesians 5:21 _____

h)   Colossians 3:16 _____

i)   1 Thessalonians 4:18 _____

j)   1 Thessalonians 5:11 _____

k)   Hebrews 10:25 _____

l)   James 5:16 _____

m)   James 5:16 _____

n)   1 Peter 4:9 _____

o)   1 Peter 4:10 _____

p)   1 John 3:11 _____

3.   Through **Utilizing** Your Spiritual Gifts

a)   Read 1 Peter 4:10 and answer the following questions:

(1)   How many believers have been given spiritual gifts?
_____

(2)   Who are to be the beneficiaries of our spiritual gifts?
_____

(3)   By utilizing our spiritual gifts, we become good
_____ of the manifold grace of God.

b)   Why is it important to utilizing of our spiritual gifts? (Romans 12:4-5) _____

c)   What are the spiritual gifts listed in Romans 12:6-8 that are to be used to build up the body?

(1)   _____

(2)   _____

(3)   _____

(4)   _____

(5)   _____

(6)   _____

(7)   _____

d)   How do we know which gift or gifts we have? Here are some guidelines for realizing and then utilizing your spiritual gifts.

(1)   Read the list and prayerfully analyze which activity comes the easiest for you.

(2)   Ask godly Christians what they think your gifts are.

(3)   Once you have an idea, ask the leadership of the church how you may utilize your gifts.

(4)   Learn the biblical principles, which give you guidelines for your gifts.

(5)   As you utilize your gifts in the church, ask people to evaluate the fruitfulness of them. This is a way to confirm where your gifts are.

Assignment: *Memorize Hebrews 10:24-25*
Complete the following review on the next page:

Complete the following review on the church.

1. After you have received Christ as your Lord and Savior, what is the other requirement that you must fulfill before becoming a member of a New Testament local church (Acts 2:41)?

2. Whom did God establish as the overseers of the local church (Acts 20:17-18; 1 Timothy 3:1-5)

3. What are some of the responsibilities of a member of a New Testament church?

    a. Acts 1:8

    b. Matthew 28:19-20

    c. Hebrews 10:24-25

4. Do you know and understand you spiritual gifts (Romans 12:6-8)?

5. Do you know how to use your spiritual gifts within the local church?

6 The Lord's Table
Remembering Our Lord

A special celebration that the church is to partake of is the Lord's Table or Communion. There are many questions surrounding this celebration:

1) **Why** is the Lord's Table important,
2) **What** is the purpose in celebrating the Lord's Table and
3) **When** is it to be celebrated?

This lesson will examine these questions in the light of biblical truth.

I.   THE IMPORTANCE OF THE LORD'S TABLE

We see the importance of the Lord's Table in the fact that:

A.   It is important because our Lord commanded it. He told the disciples, "_____ *this in remembrance of Me*" (1 Corinthians 11:23-34).

B.   It is important because the first Church practiced it. It was the church's custom on the first day of the week to come together and _____ _____ (Acts 20:7). The breaking of bread referred to the Lord's Table (see 1 Corinthians 10:16).

II.   THE PURPOSE OF THE LORD'S TABLE

While there are religions that teach that the Lord's Table is a way to partake of the actual sacrifice of Christ, the purpose is very clearly defined.

A.   It is a **Memorial**

Jesus commanded us to *"Do this in _____ of Me"* (1 Corinthians 11:23-34).

B.   It is a **Symbol**

The bread and wine were to picture the disciples partaking of Jesus _____ and _____ which were given in His sacrifice (1 Corinthians 11:24-25). Jesus did not literally become the bread and wine, any more than He literally became a door (John 10:7) or a vine (John 15:1). This symbol reminds the believer that they are saved because of the broken body and shed blood of Jesus!

Further, Jesus is not offered again and again at the Lord's Table. It is a symbol and not an actual offering of the body and blood of Christ. In 1 Peter 3:18, we are told that Jesus was offered _____ for sins.

The Lord's Table is also intended to symbolize the truth that those who believe in Christ are all part of one _____ (1 Corinthians 10:17). In 1 Corinthians 10:16, the Lord's Table is called _____. The word *"communion"* literally means "fellowship." When we partake of the Lord's Table, we symbolize our unity as a church in the truth that we have all partaken of the sacrifice of Christ.

C.   It is a **Proclamation**

We are told that every time we partake of the Lord's Table we are _____ the death of Christ (1 Corinthians 11:26).

D.   It is a **Reminder**

Every time we partake of the Lord's Table, we are reminded that this is only a temporary celebration, for we only partake of the Lord's Table until He _____ (1 Corinthians 11:26).

E.   It is a Time for **Examination**

We are not to partake of the Lord's Table in an _____ manner (1 Corinthians 11:27). We partake of the Lord's Table unworthily when we have not accepted the sacrifice of Christ, but demonstrate outwardly that we have.

During the time of the Lord's Table, each person is to examine _____ (1 Corinthians 11:28).

III.   THE TIME AND PLACE OF THE LORD'S TABLE

A.   The **Time**

There was no set pattern as to when the church was to celebrate the Lord's Table. Some do it every Sunday, others once a month. All we are told to partake _____ _____ _____ we drink it (1 Corinthians 11:25).

B.   The **Place**

The Lord's Table is to be participated by the local church body when they gather (1 Corinthians 11:18, 20).

This is why the first church knew nothing about private communion. It was always done as a church (see Acts 20:7). Also, to partake of a private communion robs the picture of common fellowship (1 Corinthians 10:16).

Assignment: *Read Matthew 26:1-35; Luke 22:1-30*

7 Testing

Persevering for Our Lord

Testings of the Christian life comes from two different directions. First, there are testings from **outside** of ourselves, which are called **trials**. Secondly, there are testings from **within**. These are called **temptations**. Both trials and temptations test the strength, maturity, and sometimes even the reality of our faith. Many Christians stop serving and living for Christ because of trials or temptations shipwrecking their faith.

This study is designed to equip the believer for those times of testings; testings from without and testings from within.

I.   TRIALS: Testings from Without

    A.   The Surety of Trials

        1.   In James 1:2, it does not say "if" the Christian has a trial, but _____.

        2.   In 2 Timothy 3:12, it says that *"all who desire to live godly in Christ Jesus* _____ *suffer persecution."*

        3.   In 1 Peter 4:12 we are told not to think of the trial as _____.

    B.   The Source of Trials

    There are a number of possible sources from where trails come into personal life.

        1.   Satan

            a)   According to Paul, who was inflicting him with his trial (2 Corinthians 12:7)? _____ _____ _____

            b)   In 1 Peter 5:8, we are told that Satan is *"seeking whom he may* _____ *"*.

            c)   In Job 1:6-12, who is it that is inflicting Job? _____

2.   Unbelievers

    a)   1 Peter 4:14 tells us that another way we may suffer insults or reproach because we were telling others about _____.

    b)   It was the *"Jews who were not _____"* that persecuted Paul (Acts 17:5).

3.   Disobedient Christians

Hymaneus and Alexander the coppersmith were believers who were disciplined from the church at Ephesus (1 Timothy 1:20). In 2 Timothy 4:14, Paul shared that Alexander did him "_____ _____".

4.   Ourselves

Sometimes we suffer trials because of wrong actions that we had done (see 1 Peter 4:15).

C.   The Strategy for Trials

1.   James 1:2 tells us when a trial comes into our life we are to consider it all _____.

2.   1 Peter 4:13 tells us to _____ when we suffer for the cause of Christ.

How can we possibly rejoice over our trials or count them joy? We can rejoice in our trials when we remember that:

    a)   Trials teach us **humility** and **dependence** (2 Corinthians 12:7)

    b)   Trials **mature** us (James 1:2-4; Romans 5:3-4)

    c)   Trials teach us to be **satisfied** with whatever the Lord gives us; contentment (James 1:4; Job 1:21)

    d)   Trials **purify** our faith (1 Peter 1:6-9)

    e)   Trials give us opportunity to **glorify God** (Acts 16:22-25)

II.   TEMPTATIONS: Testings from Within

A.   The **Surety** of Temptation

Each believer must regard temptation as an unavoidable experience

1.   A Christian can be tempted because he has many natural desires with which to be tempted. What happens when a person claims not have a sinful nature? (1 John 1:8) _____

2.   Read 1 John 1:10 and answer whether a believer still has the capacity to sin? _____

3.   It is not sin to be tempted — it is a sin to **yield** to temptation. Who was tempted yet did not sin? (Hebrews 2:18; 4:15) _____

B.   The **Sources** of Temptation

According to James 1:13, does God ever tempt His children to do evil? _____ There are basically three sources of temptation.

1.   The **World** (1 John 2:15-17)

   a)   What is impossible to love at the same time that you love God? (see James 4:4) _____ _____

   b)   To what do the things in the world appeal? (1 John 2:16)

      (1)   _____

      (2)   _____

      (3)   _____

   c)   Can the things in this world provide eternal life? (1 John 2:17) _____

2.   The **Flesh** (James 1:14-15)

   a)   What actually provides the enticement to sin when you are tempted? (James 1:14) _____

   b)   What does sin produce if it is harbored in one's heart? (James 1:15) _____

3.   The **Devil**

   a)   What is Satan continuously doing? (1 Peter 5:8)

      _____

   b)   Why is the Christian Struggle with sin so strong? (Ephesians 6:12) _____

C.   The **Strategy** Against Temptation

1.   Is there ever a temptation that enters our life that we cannot conquer? (1 Corinthians 10:13) _____

2.   What has God provided when temptation enters our life? (1 Corinthians 10:13) _____ _____

3.   How can we cause Satan to flee? (James 4:7) _____ to God
      and _____ the Devil.

4.   What are two steps we can take to prepare for temptation? (Mark
      14:38)

      a)   _____

      b)   _____

5.   What can we do to prevent yielding to temptation? (Psalm119: 9)
      _____

6.   If we yield to temptation, what should we do? (1 John 1:9; Proverbs
      28:13) _____ and _____.

Assignment: *Memorize 1 Corinthians 10:13*

8 Obedience
Commitment to Our Lord

Every believer faces numerous decisions each day in which he must decide between doing what God wants him to do and doing what his own sinful nature desires him to do.

The reason why this seems so hard is because your old nature wars with your new nature (1 Peter 2:11). Before one becomes a Christian, there was only one master: self. When we enter into that personal relationship with Christ we become a slave to God (Romans 6:22).

Christ is Lord of every believer's life, it is vital to yield to Christ as first place in one's life (Colossians 1:18).

I.   THE CHARACTERISTICS OF OBEDIENCE

   A.   It is recognizing Christ's authority over our lives.

      1.   Who does one serve before salvation? (Romans 6:17) _____

      2.   Who is one a servant to after salvation? (Romans 6:17,22) _____

   B.   It is submitting to God's Word.

      1.   When did the Galatians believers stop running well in their spiritual life? (Galatians 5:7) _____

      2.   We are to be _____ of the Word and not _____ only. (James 1:22)

   C.   It is submitting to God's Will.

      1.   How did Christ conclude His prayer in Mark 14:36?

      _____

      2.   Some will claim to know Christ as Lord. How will Christ determine who really knew Him? (Matthew 7:21)

      _____

II.   THE COST OF OBEDIENCE (Luke 14:25-35)

In this text, Christ demonstrates the cost of being a true disciple.

    A.   Relinquish all rivals for your affections (Luke 14:26)

        1.   Which of our loved ones should we love more than Christ? _____

        2.   How about our own life? Can we hold on to that and still be a disciple of Christ? _____

    B.   Be willing to follow Christ at any cost (Luke 14:27)

        1.   What is symbolized by a cross? _____

        2.   What is true if we are not willing to die to self? _____

    C.   Renounce all personal possessions (Luke 14:33)

        1.   What must one abandon if he is to be a disciple of Christ? _____

        2.   What exceptions does Christ allow? _____

        3.   What is true if something that we own or desire is more important to us than Christ? _____

III.   THE CRITERIA FOR OBEDIENCE (Romans 12:1-2)

    A.   Complete surrender of self to Christ (Romans 12:1)

        1.   What does God want to make of our bodies? _____

        2.   What should motivate us to take that step? _____

        3.   What kind of sacrifice does God desire? _____

        4.   Is that an unreasonable demand? _____

    B.   Daily separation from the pattern of the world (Romans 12:2)

        1.   What is the wrong pattern for the Christian's life?

            _____

        2.   How is the world attempting to impose its standards on your life?

            _____

C.   Constant change from self-centered living to Christ-centered living (Romans 12:2)

1.   How does this transformation take place? (see also 2 Corinthians 4:16)
      _____

2.   What needs to be renewed in order for this transformation to take place? _____

3.   When our life is transforming, what will become clear to us?
      _____

4.   What do we know about the will of God?

      It is   G_____

               A_____

               P_____

5.   What do we do in situations that the Bible does not specifically address?

      We need to ask these questions:

      a)   Does it glorify God? (1 Corinthians 10:31)

      b)   Are the things in question doubtful? (Romans 14:23)

      c)   Will this activity cause another to stumble? (1 Corinthians 8:12-13)

      d)   Will it enslave me? (1 Corinthians 6:12)

      e)   Does it build me up spiritually, mentally, or physically? (1 Corinthians 10:23)

      f)   Is this habit, person, or situation worldly? (1 John 2:15-17)

      g)   Would I want my children to follow my example? (Galatians 6:7)

      h)   Does it harm my body? (1 Corinthians 6:19,20)

      i)   May I do this activity and still be controlled by the Holy Spirit? (Ephesians 5:18)

IV.   THE CATALYST FOR OBEDIENCE

    A.   The two greatest commandments hinge on a _____ for God and a _____ for others (Matthew 22:36-40).

    B.   Jesus said that we will be obedient to Him if we really _____ Him (John 14:15).

    C.   We demonstrate a true love for our brothers and sisters in Christ, if we first _____ God and keep His _____ (1 John 5:2).

Assignment: *Memorize Romans 12:1-2*

9 Holiness

Living like Our Lord

The word "holy" means to "separate oneself from all that God calls sin". In the Bible, there are things, we as believers, are to separate ourselves.

I.   BE SEPARATE FROM THE WORLD

Worldliness is conforming to the pattern of the world (Romans 12:1-2). God's standard for His children is **holiness**. Whenever we deviate from His standard and conform to the world's that is worldliness.

A.   How does becoming a Christian affect a person's way of living? (2 Corinthians 5:17) _____

     1.   What *"old things"* have been taken away since you received Christ Jesus as your Savior?

     2.   What *"new things"* have taken their place?

B.   What happens when a Christian tries to become a friend to the godless system of this world? (James 4:4) _____

C.   What is true about any person who claims to be saved but loves the world? (1 John 2:15) _____

D.   List the three categories into which everything that the world offers you falls (1 John 2:16)

     1.   _____

     2.   _____

     3.   _____

E.   What provides the wrong pattern for a Christian's use of his body? (Romans 12:2) _____ _____

II.   BE SEPARATE FROM FALSE DOCTRINE

A.   What is the standard for sound doctrine? (2 Timothy 3:16) _____

B.   What do false teachers bring in to the church? (2 Peter 2:1)

    _____   _____

C.   What is the ultimate end of false teachers? (2 Peter 2:1)

    _____   _____

D.   What is the source of false doctrine? (1 Timothy 4:1-2) _____

E.   How do we detect false doctrine? (1 John 4:1-2) _____

F.   What should be our response when we detect false teaching? (Galatians 1:6,9; Romans 16:17-18; 2 John 7-11) _____

III.   BE SEPARATE FROM UNDISCIPLNED CHRISTIANS

A.   How should we deal with believers who stir up trouble within the church? (Romans 16:17-20; Titus 3:9-11) _____

B.   What should be the church's response toward believers who practice worldly habits? (1 Corinthians 5:9-13) _____

C.   How should we deal with believers whose lives are undisciplined and whose conduct harms their testimony for Christ? (2 Thessalonians 3:6-15)

    _____

IV.   BE SEPARATE UNTO GOD

A.   To what did the Thessalonians believers turn to when they turned away from idols? (1 Thessalonians 1:9) _____

B.   Once we separate from sin and those who are sinners, what does God say He will be to us? (2 Corinthians 6:14-18) _____

Assignment: *Memorize: 1 Peter 1:15-16*
Make a personal list of those things which render you from being holy and close to God.

10 Stewardship
Offerings for Our Lord

The area of financial stewardship is the area that critics most often attack. Yet the Bible speaks a great deal about money. The word "stewardship" simply means "management". What our attitude is toward our finances and how we handle them as Christians is very important to God.

I.   OUR ATTITUDE TOWARD MONEY

    A.   Why is our attitude toward money so important to God?

        1.   Matthew 6:24 _____

        2.   Matthew 6:21 _____

        3.   1 Timothy 6:9-10 _____

    B.   What should be out attitude toward money?

        1.   We should seek first the _____ _____ _____
            (Matthew 6:33).

        2.   What should our attitude be toward the possessions God has given us
            beyond the basic necessities? (1 Timothy 6:17-19)
            _____

        3.   What type of riches should we be primarily concerned about?
            (Proverbs 11:4; Matthew 6:19, 20) _____

        4.   God provides the _____ for His people (Proverbs 10:3;
            Matthew 6:31-32).

        5.   It is better to have little and have:

            Proverbs 15:16 _____

            Proverbs 15:17 _____

            Proverbs 16:8 _____

            Proverbs 17:1 _____

Proverbs 19:1 _____

Proverbs 22:1 _____

C.   What should our attitude **not** be toward money?

        1.   We should not look at employment simply as a way to _____ (Proverbs 23:3-4).

        2.   We should not _____ in riches (Proverbs 11:28)

        3.   We should not _____ riches (Proverbs 27:20; Hebrews 13:5)

II.   OUR PROCUREMENT OF MONEY

      A.   Improper Procurement

        1.   We should not use _____ to obtain money (Proverbs 20:17; 21:6)

        2.   We should not obtain money through _____ (Proverbs 13:11) *"Vanity"* simply means not working hard for it.

        3.   We should not _____ to obtain money (Ephesians 4:28).

      B.   Proper Procurement

        1.   In what is there profit? (Proverbs 14:23) _____

        2.   What hinders us from laboring?

            Proverbs 14:23 _____

            Proverbs 20:13 _____

            Proverbs 6:6-10 _____

III.   OUR USE OF MONEY

      A.   We are to _____ _____ (Proverbs 14:31)

      B.   We are to take care of that which we have (Proverbs 27:23).

      C.   As a steward, we are to be _____ (1 Corinthians 4:2).

      D.   If a man does not work, he should not _____ (2 Thessalonians 3:10).

E.   1 Thessalonians 4:11-12 give two reasons why a Christian should work (especially verse 12).

      1.   _____

      2.   _____

IV.   OUR GIVING OF MONEY

While many people abuse this teaching of Scripture, it is clear that Christians are to support their local church.

A.   The Place for Giving

In the New Testament, giving was always in relationship to the local church.

    1.   Acts 4:32-37   Church of Jerusalem

    2.   Acts 11:26-30   Church of Antioch

    3.   1 Corinthians 16:1   Church of Galatia

    4.   1 Corinthians 16:1-4   Church in Corinth

    5.   1 Corinthians 8:1-5   Church of Macedonia

    6.   Philippians 4:15-16   Church of Philippi

B.   The Reason for Giving

Notice in these texts the use of finances as they relate to the local church.

    1.   Support of pastoral staff (1 Corinthians 9:13-14; 1 Timothy 5:17-18).

    2.   Help to the needy (Acts 4:32-35)

    3.   Missionary support (Philippians 4:15-16)

    4.   For the overall ministry of the church.

C.   The Method of Giving

In 1 Corinthians 16:1-4 Paul is instructing the church at Corinth in how to give for the special project of relief for the poverty-stricken Christians in Jerusalem. Notice the following principles that can apply to giving:

    1.   **Regular** giving   *"upon the first day of the week"*

    2.   **Worshipful** giving   *"first day of the week'*

    3.   **Personal** giving   *"let every one of you"*

    4.   **Proportionate** giving   *"as God has prospered"*

God does not demand a certain percentage of a Christian's income and possessions. However, His Word does provide helping establishing guidelines for our proportionate giving.

    a)   **Minimum** proportion in the Bible is a tenth (Genesis 14:20; 28:22)

    b)   **Maximum** proportion in the Bible is 100% (Luke 21:1-4).

D.   The Attitude in Giving – 2 Corinthians 9:6-15

1.   God desires a **generous** attitude (9:6)

2.   God desires a **joyful** attitude (9:7)

3.   God desires a **trusting** attitude (9:8-11)

4.   God desires a **thankful** attitude (9:14,15)

Notice that our motivation to give in this way is the exceeding grace of God in our life.

Assignment: *Read 2 Corinthians 8 and 9*

11 Evangelism
Speaking for Our Lord

Telling others about what God has done for us is often difficult. Yet, if we really believe what we believe, it is vital for believers to be witnesses for Christ.

I.   THE MEANING OF EVANGELISM

      A.   It is bringing people to Christ (John 1:41-42).

      B.   Christ compared it to _____ (Matthew 4:19). What does this verse say we are fishing for? _____

II.   THE MOTIVATION TO EVANGELISM

      A.   Who has called believers to be witnesses? _____ (Matthew 4:19; 28:19-20; Acts 1:8)

      B.   Who is our example? _____ (John 3:1-7; 4:1-26)

      C.   Notice the example of early Christians:

            1.   Andrew (John 1:40-42)

            2.   Apostles in Jerusalem (Acts 5:42)

            3.   Christians in Jerusalem (Acts 8:1, 4)

            4.   Stephen (Acts 7)

            5.   Philip (Acts 8:5; 26-40)

            6.   Paul and Silas (Acts 16:13-15)

      D.   What is the condition of those who do not believe? (John 3:18, 36)

            _____

      E.   What is God's commandment for those who are not saved? (Acts 17:30; 2 Peter 3:9) _____

      F.   How are they to hear about salvation? (Romans 10:13-17) _____

      G.   What should constrain (compel) us to witness? (2 Corinthians 5:14)

            _____

III.   THE MESSAGE IN EVANGELISM

A.   Explain that they are sinners (Romans 3:10, 23).

How many does God say are good? _____

How many are sinners? _____

B.   Explain that their sin brings the penalty of death (Romans 6:23).

1.   **Spiritual** death (Ephesians 2:1,5)

2.   **Physical** death (Genesis 5:5)

3.   **Eternal** death (Revelation 20:11-15; 21:8)

Remembering that death in Scripture simply means separation. Spiritual separation is the condition of a man from his physical birth until his spiritual birth. Physical death is a man's soul separating from his body. Eternal death is that separation for all eternity.

C.   Explain that they cannot save themselves by their heritage, works or anything else that they trust (Ephesians 2:8-9; Titus 3:5; Romans 4:4).

D.   Explain to them that Christ can save them.

1.   He died to pay the penalty for their _____ (Romans 5:8; 1 Corinthians 15:3).

2.   He resurrected from the dead (1 Corinthians 15:4; Romans 10:9-10).

3.   He is _____ over all (Romans 14:11, 12; see also Acts 4:12).

E.   Explain their need to receive Christ.

1.   They need to repent of their sin and turn from whatever they were trusting for salvation (Luke 24:47; Acts 17:30; 2 Peter 3:9).

2.   They need to _____ Christ (John 1:12; Romans 10:9-10, 13).

a)   Receive Christ as **Savior** – The One who will save them from their sin.

b)   Receive Christ as **Lord** – Because that is His rightful place.

F.   Some practical suggestions

    1.   Be sure they understand how to be saved.

    2.   Ask them if they would like to be saved.

    3.   Ask them to pray:

        a)   Admitting their sinfulness

        b)   Asking Christ to save them

        c)   Affirming Christ's Lordship over them

        d)   Affirming their belief in His death and resurrection

        e)   Repenting from their sin and their trust in self for salvation

IV.   ANSWERING COMMON EXCUSES

A.   "I am a good person" (Romans 3:10,23; Revelation 21:8; James 2:10)

B.   "Not now, some other time" (Proverbs 27:1; 2 Corinthians 6:2)

C.   "I don't feel ready" (Ephesians 2:8-9; John 6:37).

D.   "Too much to give up" (Matthew 6:33; Revelation 20:11-15)

E.   "I am afraid I can't live it" (Galatians 2:20; Philippians 1:6; 2:14)

F.   "I am sincere in my belief" (Proverbs 14:12; Matthew 7:13-14)

G.   "God is love, He would not damn anyone or send anyone to hell' (Matthew 25:41, 46; Revelation 20:10-15)

H.   "I don't believe there is a hell" (Luke 16:19-30; Revelation 20:10; 21:8)

I.   "I'll have a second chance" (Hebrews 9:27; Luke 16:19-30)

J.   "I am very religious" (Titus 3:5; Galatians 2:16; Ephesians 2:8-9)

K.   "I'm too great a sinner' (1 Timothy 1:15; Isaiah 1:18; Luke 23)

L.   "My friends and relatives won't understand" (Matthew 10:32-38; 2 Timothy 2:12)

M.   "I have always been a Christian, I was born one" (John 1:12; 3:3; Ephesians 2:1-3; 2 Corinthians 5:17)

N.   "I believe death ends all" (Luke 12:4-5; Hebrews 9:27; Revelation 20:11-15)

O.   "How do we know there is a god?" (Psalm 19:1-6; Romans 1:19-20; 2 Timothy 3:16).

P.   "How do you know that the Bible is true?" (2 Timothy 3:16)

Assignment: *Memorize the Five Point Message of Salvation and a Scripture reference for each point.*

12 Christian Home
Legacy for Our Lord

Whether you are part of a family or not, the Christian home is vital for the handing down of our faith in Christ to the next generation. The institution of the family was very important to God. In this study, we will examine the basic guidelines for the family as well as address some of the principles concerning the Christian and singleness.

I.   GUIDELINES FOR CHRISTIAN FAMILIES

    A.   The Institution (Genesis 2:23-24)

       Marriage is a very special institution in the eyes of God. It was through the institution of marriage that life would be procreated, loneliness would be prevented, Christ's love for the church would be pictured and the truths of Christianity would be promoted. Notice these truths about the institution of marriage.

       1.   Marriage is to **Monogamous**.

         It is _____ which shall become _____ flesh (Genesis 2:24; Mark 10:8)

       2.   Marriage is to be **Heterosexual**.

         A _____ shall leave his father and mother and cleave to his _____ (Genesis 2:24).

       3.   Marriage is to be **Permanent**.

         Was divorce ever part of God's perfect design for marriage? _____ (Matthew 19:8)

         "What God has put together, let not man _____ " (Mark 10:9).

         "For the LORD God of Israel says that He _____ divorce" (Malachi 2:16 NKJV).

    B.   The Husband

       1.   A husband is to _____ his wife (Ephesians 5:25).

         What is the pattern? *"just as _____ loved the _____ "*

2.   A husband is to love his wife as _____ (Ephesians 5:33).

3.   A husband is to be the _____ of the household (Ephesians 5:23).

      This does not mean that the husband is the **authoritarian**, but the **example** for the family in spiritual life, ministry, love, honesty, giving, and respect. He is the one responsible before God for the decisions and the directions of the family.

4.   A husband is to dwell with his wife with _____, is to give _____ to his wife, and is to consider her as an _____ together of the grace of life (1 Peter 3:7).

5.   If a husband does not fulfill the above responsibilities, does God hear his prayers? _____ (1 Peter 3:7)

6.   A husband is not to be _____ toward his wife (Colossians 3:19).

C.   The Wife

1.   God made the wife as a _____ for the man (Genesis 2:18; 1 Corinthians 11:9).

2.   A wife is to _____ herself to her own husband (Ephesians 5:22).

      a)   This is to be done in _____ (Ephesians 5:24).

      b)   The only exception is when you must obey _____ rather than _____ (Acts 5:29).

3.   A wife is to _____ her husband (Ephesians 5:33).

4.   A wife should have a _____ conduct coupled with _____ (1 Peter 3:2). Note that this fear is not toward the husband but toward the Lord.

5.   A wife should have a _____ and _____ spirit. This is very _____ in the sight of God (1 Peter 3:4).

D.   The Children

1.   Their **Responsibilities**

      a)   Children are commanded to _____ their parents (Ephesians 6:1).

      b)   Children are to _____ in all things (Colossians 3:20).

c)   Children are to _____ their father and mother (Exodus 20:12).

2.   **Their Instruction**

a)   A child can know the _____ _____ when they are young (2 Timothy 3:15).

b)   Whose responsibility is it to bring children up in the nurture and admonition of the Lord? _____ (Ephesians 6:4)

c)   Parents are to teach the Word of God _____ to their children (Deuteronomy 6:7).

d)   Some practical suggestions for Family Bible time:

(1)   Set aside a time each day (i.e., after dinner, bedtime).

(2)   Depending on age of children, read a portion of the Bible, a children's Bible, or have them read, if they are able.

(3)   Sing songs or choruses geared to the ages of your children.

(4)   Have each child that is able (2 or older) pray. Give them something specific to pray for.

3.   **Their Correction**

a)   Fathers are not to _____ their children to _____ (Ephesians 6:4).

Why should a father not provoke his children? (Colossians 3:21) _____ _____

b)   Parents are, however, commanded to _____ withhold correction from a child (Proverbs 23:13).

c)   If a parent loves their child they will discipline them _____ (Proverbs 13:24).

This literally means "early", while they are impressionable.

d)   We must discipline while there is _____ (Proverbs 19:18).

e)   What is God's method for disciplining a child? _____ _____ (Proverbs 23:14).

The *"rod"* was a switch, which stung without injuring. Spanking is never to be done in anger. Rather, it is only to be done for acts or attitudes of clear disobedience, and is only done enough to correct the problem.

f) _____ is bound up in the heart of the child and the _____ of correction will drive it from him (Proverbs 22:15).

Note that *"foolishness"* is not childishness, but knowing what is right and **NOT** doing it!

g) A child left to themselves, without correction, will bring _____ to their mother (Proverbs 29:15).

h) A child who is lovingly and consistently corrected gives a parent _____ and _____ for the soul (Proverbs 29:17).

II.   GUIDELINES FOR CHRISTIAN SINGLENESS

A.   The Perspective of Singleness

It is _____ if an unmarried or widowed person remains single (1 Corinthians 7:8). If being single is God's calling for you at this time, you must recognize that this is best.

B.   The Benefits of Singleness

1.   Paul recommended singleness would be good because of the present _____ (1 Corinthians 7:26).

2.   A person who is unmarried can care for the things of the _____ and how they may please Him (1 Corinthians 7:32).

3.   The person is _____ by the law as long as their spouse lives. It is because of this truth that singles should NOT rush into a marriage.

C.   The Dangers of Singleness

1.   **Immorality**

What is the remedy for one who is unable to control their sexual desires? _____ (1 Corinthians 7:9).

2.   *Wrong Decision*

What is the limitation on whom a Christian may marry? _____ (1 Corinthians 7:39)

D. Some practical suggestions:

Below is a list of practical suggestions to keep yourself pure (from John MacArthur's *Guidelines for Singleness and Marriage*, pages 52-53).

1. Channel your energy through physical work and spiritual ministry.

2. Do not seek to be married for the sake of being married.

3. Let go of the sex-mad, adulterous world.

4. Program your mind with the Word of God.

5. Count on Divine enablement to live without sexual fulfillment (pray).

6. Avoid potentially tempting situations.

7. Praise and thank God in the midst of your singleness.

8. Be accountable to a close friend of the same sex.

Assignment: *Memorize:* *Husbands – Ephesians 5:25*
Wives – Ephesians 5:22
Children – Ephesians 6:1
Singles – 1 Corinthians 7:24

www.ingramcontent.com/pod-product-compliance
Lightning Source LLC
Chambersburg PA
CBHW080552030426
42337CB00024B/4848